The Continuing Journey

The Continuing Journey

Stewardship and useful case studies in philanthropy

William T. Sturtevant

a companion to *The Artful Journey*

Bonus Books, Inc.

05   04   03   02   01   5   4   3   2   1

Library of Congress Control Number: 00-109842
ISBN: 1-56625-159-1

Bonus Books, Inc.
160 East Illinois Street
Chicago, Illinois 60611

Printed in the United States of America

My thanks to all of my mentors and colleagues who have shared freely of their experience and wisdom. I would also like to thank the many donors with whom I have been privileged to work. They have enriched my life immeasurably, and their generosity has inspired me. These donors are making a tremendous difference in the quality of life for others, and it is an honor to be associated with them. In many cases, they have become dear and cherished life-long friends. Most importantly, I want to thank my family for providing me a foundation of love. My journey continues to be the richest one imaginable.

— W.T.S.

Table of Contents

Introduction

When I wrote *The Artful Journey* a few years ago I had no idea the impact it would have. I have heard from many thoughtful and valued colleagues about the effect it has had on their major gifts fundraising efforts, and I am indebted to those who took time to communicate with me. My hope was to make a difference to organizations which serve and enrich all of us, and it pleases me to know that this might be the case.

The concepts and precepts examined in *The Artful Journey* were acquired through experience, the graceful sharing by colleagues and mentors, and, not insignificantly, through trial and error. As to the latter, you can be certain that I have made just about every conceivable misstep in fundraising. I trust and hope that I have learned in the process.

After completing *The Artful Journey,* the feedback received from my numerous seminars and presentations told me that two additional topics are relevant to our success in securing significant gift commitments. While these topics were touched upon in my first book, they merit more extensive treatment. The good news is that there is much to be shared.

A topic of undeniable importance is that of stewardship. I continued my cogitations and research on the topic and discovered that some tools and concepts can truly make a difference. This includes a means of testing how well we are doing as an organization in providing good stewardship. The concepts were tested in the seminar context and the response has been overwhelmingly positive. Hence, our discussion of stewardship. I hope you find it valuable.

One of the most useful experiences at our fundraising seminars has been the sharing of actual cases. Case studies allow the fundraiser the opportunity to hone analytical and strategic skills. I thought it was critical that the cases be real in order to render them relevant, although, of course, the names have been changed in order to guard identities. With some of the cases in this book, there have been slight alterations of the scenarios, but where this has occurred the basic dynamics remain untouched. The point to be made is that all of the cases are real and therefore relevant to our objectives. I think you will agree that the cases are a wonderful tool whether used alone or in a group setting. After all, they pertain to the daily challenges of the major gift fundraiser. The inclusion of outcomes in the last section of the book will allow you to test your concepts for rigor and completeness, although it should always be remembered that there is no single path to the same successful outcome.

This volume is intended to supplement *The Artful Journey* in a meaningful way. That's why we have entitled it *The Continuing Journey*. It can also be read as a stand-alone for those who particularly wish to benefit from case studies and focus on the critical topic of stewardship. I sincerely hope you and the organization you represent will be able to utilize the concepts as building blocks toward greater success in serving important objectives.

Good luck in your artful and continuing journey on behalf of the causes you represent. I can think of no higher calling nor more exciting profession than that of fundraising. And it is, indeed, a journey. It is one in which you should take great joy. Stevenson said, "It is a better thing to travel hopefully than to arrive." May you travel hopefully and successfully.

William T. Sturtevant
July 2000

I

Stewardship and the Good Giving Experience

"To give away money is an easy matter and in anyone's power. But to decide to whom to give it and how large and when, and for what purpose and how, is neither in *every* person's power—nor an easy matter. Hence it is that such excellence is rare, praiseworthy and noble."

Aristotle

Andrew Carnegie once said that "It is more difficult to give money away intelligently than it is to earn it in the first place." I suspect he was correct. Our donors wish to have an impact through their giving, and to that they are certainly entitled. Demonstrating just how a gift achieves the desired impact is the essence of the stewardship process.

Some years ago at one of our major gifts seminars we were fortunate to have Stanley Marcus, cofounder of Nieman-Marcus, attend as a special guest. Stanley and my partner, Jerold Panas, had forged a strong friendship, a fact we used to good advantage by asking Stanley to spend some time with the fundraisers in attendance. What a special human being he is. Stanley has long recognized the importance of good stewardship in any transactional relationship, as evidenced by what he once said about Nieman-Marcus customers. His observation was that "There is never a good sale for Nieman-Marcus unless it's a good buy for the customer." How right he was. As fundraisers we should always remember that it is never a good gift for our donors unless they receive the satisfaction to which they are entitled.

Stewardship is critical for two reasons. First, it is our fiduciary responsibility to ensure that donors' gifts are handled properly. They must be used for the designated purposes, and the judicious application of entrusted gift funds is vital. Where investing is involved, as is true with endowments, responsible actions and prudence in this regard are mandatory. Finally, our donors must be receipted properly for tax purposes.

The second aspect of stewardship, and the one deemed most important to fundraisers, is that of using stewardship as a cultivational tool. We have already stated that the best cultivation is the good giving experience, and this is truly what stewardship is all about. If we do our jobs well, each gift begets the next commitment because we provide our donors with a good giving experience.

Effective stewardship carries our donors to a higher motivational plane. I think of this in regard to a major benefactor with whom I was associated many years ago. While attending a luncheon to celebrate the issuance of the first fellowship made possible by his generous support, this donor made a startling confession. Here is what he said.

> "Bill, when you first approached me I had a tax problem. You listened and solved my problem, which is the reason I made the gift to your cause. But I must confess that I would have made the gift to any other charitable organization which happened to approach me and help me solve my problem. However, now that I have met this fellowship recipient I would make the gift even if there were no tax savings involved. This whole experience has added ten years to my life."

That's pretty powerful stuff. It's the sort of satisfaction we should seek for all of our donors, and stewardship plays a key role.

There is a term in marketing called "aftermarketing," and what it refers to is stewardship as it pertains to customers. It has great relevance for the fundraising counterpart. Much of the section to follow owes its existence to an insightful book called *Aftermarketing* by Terry G. Vavra.

The essence of stewardship is providing continuing satisfaction and reinforcement to current or past donors. Donors to our organizations must be tracked, communicated with, acknowledged, responded to and periodically audited for satisfaction. The ultimate goal of stewardship is to build lasting relationships with donors by ensuring that their expectations regarding the giving experience are met.

Research and common sense tells us that our donors' perception of the quality of the exchange or giving relationship is a key factor in building long-term connections which are positive. Our goal is to increase loyalty and satisfaction. Accomplishing this entails gaining an understanding of how our donors will assess the quality of their giving experience with our organization. The idea is to provide evidence to our donors that their gifts are achieving the desired purpose and that we are grateful as a result. We provide this evidence in many ways. Among the ways to demonstrate the impact of a gift, and thereby help ensure satisfaction, are the following:

- Plaques
- Certificates
- Fund agreements (see *Artful Journey*)
- Interactions with the beneficiaries of the organization's services (e.g. students and patients)

- Acknowledgement letters (and plenty of them!)
- Receipts (timely, as in 24 to 36 hours!)
- Interactions with fundraisers, staff members and volunteers
- Recognition at events and in publications

Two psychiatrists, Zoonan and Zoonan, postulate that there is a short moment in time, a window of opportunity of approximately four minutes, during which the satisfaction of the human contact will either be established or denied. That's actually a rather frightening thought. The two researchers describe good contacts in terms of the "four C's":

- Confidence — at least one of the parties must convey a certain degree of self-confidence.
- Creativity — one must find a way to tune into the feelings of the other party.
- Caring — it's important to demonstrate personal interest and total attention.
- Consideration — this entails being sensitive, aware and a good listener.

Even if Zoonan and Zoonan have understated the time available for the establishment of a good connection, it is obvious that fundraisers must assess all of the contact points with donors. I can tell you from personal experience that gift satisfaction can be quickly tarnished by an organizational representative who conveys the wrong message.

Stewardship is the consistent delivery of services which fully meet donors' needs and expectations. Managing the process of stewardship entails the following steps:

- Identifying donors' possible contact points with organizational representatives.
- Instructing and motivating staff (i.e., the contact points) as to how to satisfy the donors.
- Monitoring the quality of donors' experiences and taking corrective actions as necessary.

As fundraisers interested in stewardship, we must reconcile what our donors expect with what they actually receive. Two social/psychological theories may help you in this endeavor. The first is called *consistency theory*. This suggests that expectations may actually be more important than performance. The reason this is so is that donors will try to avoid inconsistencies by shaping their perceptions of reality to their expectations. In other words, if expectations are positive, donors will work very hard to perceive their experience as satisfactory. When this dynamic is at work you may not need to worry about over-promising because the more they expect the more likely they are to view their experiences as reinforcing. To a certain extent the good experience becomes a self-fulfilling prophecy. I have seen cases where certain occurrences would have injured the relationship between the donor and the organization had they occurred earlier in the process. However, this did not occur because the donor had convinced himself or herself that the organization was wonderful and, therefore, minor aggravations or missteps along the way were not deemed critical. This is consistency theory in action.

The other behavioral theory of importance is termed *assimilation and contrast*. This is where our donors either exaggerate (contrast) or minimize (assimilate) the differences between their experiences and expectations. In some cases the more involved the donor is with the organization, the more likely he or she is to demand the exact level of satisfaction which is expected. With these involved donors, small shortfalls can be exaggerated. However, with other donors the shortfalls are minimized. Haven't you had cases where some donors have a greatly exaggerated response to a perceived slight, where as other donors don't seem nearly as upset as they should be? I know I have. This is the assimilation and contrast theory in operation. They are opposing reactions to the same stimulus, and it can be difficult to predict which will surface with a given donor. But we know this occurs and it helps us to interpret and understand a given reaction.

The point of explaining these theories is to assist us in gaining a greater understanding of complex human dynamics such that we can better deal with and react to our donors' reactions. It should also help us formulate possible responses and help guide our communications.

How well does your organization do in the stewardship area? It is probably safe to conclude that it is not doing as well as it could be, and I say this because I believe this is true for most of us. Stewardship has just not received the attention it deserves. Jerry Panas and I developed a test to help organizations determine how well they are doing in this vital function. We call it the stewardship inventory. I have reproduced the stewardship inventory questionnaire in the next section. It would be time well spent for you and other development professionals in your organization to apply the test to your organization.

I must hasten to caution that you should not feel too discouraged with a low score. Most organizations woefully underachieve in stewardship. It should steel you to begin implementing a strong stewardship program, and one benefit of the inventory is to remind us of the areas which require attention.

To assist you in deciding on an effective stewardship program for your organization, you can benchmark similar organizations which seem to be more effective in this area. It seems to me that the organization which is effective at stewardship will display the following characteristics:

- **Donor services are designed to maximize satisfaction with the giving relationship.** This seems obvious, but I have observed that many services are inadequately perceived and performed. It is not unusual for organizations to send out a timely and attractive gift receipt, and yet be slipshod about providing endowment reports as to both investment performance and application. All service and communication points should be monitored and managed.

- **The organization which is effective at stewardship ensures that donor expectations are understood and managed**. When a charitable organization is effective at stewardship you can be sure that the fundraising staff is donor focused. The staff understands what donors hope for from the giving relationship and there is an assiduous effort to ensure that this is achieved. In organizations which are effective at stewardship there seems to be an almost obsessive desire on the part of staff to learn what donors want.

- **If an organization is effective at stewardship you can be certain that there are incredibly high standards of performance for all who are involved in the process.** These high standards not only apply to fundraisers, but also to accountants, clerks and others who help receipt and acknowledge.

- **The effective organization devotes energy and resources to stewardship.** This is manifested by the inclusion of stewardship in plans and discussions. A very meaningful manifestation of a commitment to stewardship is in separate and adequate budgeting for the process.

- **In high performing organizations, stewardship is considered to be the business of all employees, not just the fundraisers.**

- **In an effective organization personnel are hired, trained and motivated with stewardship in mind.** Take a look at some job descriptions. Are stewardship activities included and emphasized?

- **Where an organization is committed to stewardship its donors are consistently asked to**

weigh their experiences. This can be done through focus groups, surveys or by actively soliciting anecdotal evidence from field personnel.

Sometimes a worthy endeavor in an attempt to improve stewardship services is to visit dissatisfied donors. Here's why paying some attention to disgruntled donors may reap handsome rewards.

- With rare exceptions, donors do not totally abandon an organization due to a moderately dissatisfying experience. They may be accessible and responsive. Sometimes the mere act of your expressing an interest in the cause of dissatisfaction brings someone back into the fold. In cases where donors are totally dissatisfied, the information you learn may help you improve the organization's performance and preclude mishaps in the future. But more often than not, you stand a good chance of getting a donor to return. And once they do, they often return as roaring advocates. Exploring the source of dissatisfaction will help immeasurably. My friend and colleague, Jerold Panas, is fond of reminding us that it is good to invite expressions of displeasure. He cautions us not to worry too much about negative expressions, and he illustrates this by quoting Mark Twain, who said of Wagner's music, "It's not as bad as it sounds."

- Previous donors, although they may have moved on to greater passions or higher priorities, often retain some degree of loyalty or affinity toward the organization. By reconnecting you may just rekindle passion for the cause.

- After leaving you and experiencing a relationship with another charitable organization, a given donor may lower his or her expectations. This can be especially true where someone has unrealistic expectations to begin with. Experience with another charitable cause can render the donor a bit more realistic about what to expect from the giving relationship.

- The problem causing the original dissatisfaction may well have been ameliorated, and the reconnection with the dissatisfied donor will allow you to point this out. Where donors become convinced that this is the case, they often return to their giving ways.

Here are some possible reasons for donors to have abandoned the giving relationship with your organization.

- Dissatisfaction with your service or your responsiveness.
- Inadequate or inappropriate recognition.
- Poor handling of a complaint.
- Disapproval of organizational changes.
- Dissatisfaction with personal treatment.
- New people or policies.
- A competitive relationship appears more attractive.

I offer the above as a way for you to consider lost donors and determine if corrective actions are necessary. With disaffected donors, your task is to find out what happened, research the donor's current situation and relate it to your organization, and reestablish a relationship if a match is deemed possible.

Here are some service and stewardship elements for you to measure against. Positive ratings in these categories will guarantee your stewardship success.

- Reliability — Are you accurate and dependable in all of your communications with donors?

- Responsiveness — Do you demonstrate promptness in follow-up and communications? Do you acknowledge gifts promptly and repeatedly?

- Competence — Are you good at what you do?

- Courtesy — Do you display impeccable manners and demonstrate a desire to satisfy?

- Credibility — Are you and your organization trustworthy?

- Security/Confidentiality — Are you meticulous about maintaining confidentiality and demonstrating sensitivity about information sharing?

- Access — Is your organization and its representatives approachable and easy to contact?

- Communications — Do you communicate actively and consistently with your donors?

- Understanding Your Donors — Do you actively determine and discuss donor motivations and measure the satisfaction of your contributors?

- Tangibles — Are your facilities and materials attractive and relevant?

There may be nothing more important you can do for your organization than to help it achieve excellence in stewardship. It may also be the greatest favor you ever do for your donors. It is just that important. Obviously, it is more than a timely receipt and the seven acknowledgements Jerry Panas recommends in *Mega Gifts*, although those are undeniably important manifestations of good stewardship.

In essence, it is an attitude. Every contact point with your donors must display the appropriate attitude, and you must seek out opportunities to provide these warm, caring friends with the giving experience to which they are entitled. When you become fully committed to that end, and especially when the organization displays the same commitment, you can be sure that your donors will contribute again and at levels heretofore unimaginable. Your stewardship program provides the opportunity to carry your fundraising to the next level of success. Aristotle once said, "Quality is not an act, but a habit." For the committed fundraiser and donor-focused charitable cause, good stewardship must become a habit.

II

The 4-A
Stewardship
Inventory

"It takes a noble person to plant a tree that will one day provide shade for those whom he or she may never meet."

Author Unknown

Acquisition • Acknowledgement • Appreciation • Affinity

Research shows that it requires 4.5 times the effort, staff, and dollars to acquire a new donor as it does to keep one. Yet...some organizations seem to spend more time and energy pursuing a new giver than making the effort to keep the old friend.

We know that with proper planning (Acknowledgement and Appreciation) you can keep your donors. We have proven that with effective Stewardship (Affinity), you can be certain of very high retention and an enthusiastic donor base. If you follow systematic procedures, the program is as close to fail-proof as you can get. Securing (Acquisition) is obviously the first step. But there will be poor retention unless you acknowledge promptly and effectively, show appreciation regularly and sincerely, and give priority to winning the donor's heart and mind to the cause. These are all the components of the program you should follow.

Here is a test that will examine how effective you are in your Stewardship (maintenance) program. The instrument has been tested in the field to determine its comprehensiveness and the validation of the scoring. It was then reviewed and approved for use by the Board of Visitors of the Institute.

If it is true, and it is — that it makes more sense to keep (and increase the level of giving) of your donors—then effective Stewardship and the **4A** cycle deserves a priority of your organization's time, energy, and staff allocation.

Keeping your donors is not a matter of good luck. It means having a systematic program in place and unending attention to effective implementation. The dividends to your organization will be extraordinary.

—The Institute for Charitable Giving

Here is how to determine the effectiveness of your Stewardship 4As. Total the points you indicated in the right hand column and compare them to the table that follows:

TOTAL POINTS	YOUR STEWARDSHIP QUOTIENT
90 to 77	Outstanding — you're doing great!
76 to 63	You're doing well, but some areas still require attention.
62 to 50	Your stewardship is only fair — you could improve dramatically with some effort.
49 and below	Much additional effort is needed.

Adust the score proportionately if certain program elements (i.e., endowment fund reports) do not apply to your organization.

QUESTIONS	POINTS
1 Do you have a systematic design and plan in place, and in writing, that indicates specifically your acknowledgement and stewardship program? Yes = 3 pts. No = 0 pts.	
2 Is your stewardship plan in the form of a Manual and is it reviewed at least annually for effectiveness and relevancy? Yes = 2 pts. No = 0 pts.	
3 Does your development committee or Foundation have a subcommittee on stewardship that meets regularly? At least twice a year = 3 pts. Once a year = 1 pt. No committee = 0 pts.	
4 Does your organization issue a sufficient number of acknowledge-ment letters or thank you notes for every gift received? 7 or more = 5 pts. 5 or 6 = 4 pts. 3 or 4 = 3 pts. 2 = 1 pt. 1 only = −1 pt.	

QUESTIONS	POINTS
5 Are acknowledgement letters reviewed at least once a year and changed? Yes = 2 pts. No = 0 pts.	
6 Have you used an outside source or some of your volunteers to test the appropriateness, effectiveness, and *personal touch* of your letters? Yes = 2 pts. No = 0 pts.	
7 How long does it take your organization to send out the first acknowledgement letter after a gift is received? 24 hours = 5 pts. 48 hours = 4 pts. 72 hours = 3 pts. 96 hours = 2 pts. 5 days = 1 pt. 5–10 days = 0 pts. longer than 10 days = –2 pts.	
8 Do you issue a formal receipt, in addition to your acknowledgement letter, which can be retained by the donor for his or her tax records file? Yes = 1 pt. No = 0 pts.	

QUESTIONS	POINTS
9 Do you report outcomes and results to your donors (by personal contact, letter, or telephone) of how important their gifts were to those your organization serves? Yes = 4 pts. No = 0 pts.	
10 Do you issue financial reports to your endowment fund donors which provide investment value and performance information on their individual funds? Yes = 2 pts. No = 0 pts. Not applicable = 0 pts.	
11 If yes to #10, how often do you issue fund reports? Quarterly = 2 pts. Semi-annually = 1 pt. Annually = 0 pts.	

QUESTIONS	POINTS
12 It is highly desirable that donors have the joy and continued involvement in the gifts they make. Do you encourage agreements in your endowment funds to allow donors to create their own gift program? Yes = 3 pts. No = 0 pts. Not applicable = 0 pts.	
13 Is the payment (or notice) given to the life income recipients issued on a bank check (by the bank) or on a check or notification with the institution's name? Institution = 2 pts. Bank = 0 pts.	
14 How are the life income checks sent? Taken in person = 3 pts. Taken in person on a selective basis = 2 pts. Mailed or wired with a thank you = 1 pt. Mailed or wired = 0 pts.	

QUESTIONS	POINTS
15 In your acknowledgement program do you systematically include letters or contacts from your institution's beneficiaries— such as students, patients, campers, etc.? Yes = 3 pts.　　No = 0 pts.	
16 Do staff members or volunteers systematically call and thank individuals who donate over a certain threshold amount? Calls at $100 level = 4 pts. Calls at $1000 level or above = 1 pt. No calls = 0 pts.	
17 Does your organization publish an Annual Report which includes some sort of Honor Roll of donors? Yes = 3 pts.　　No = 0 pts.	
18 In the Honor Roll, do you indicate the number of years of continuous giving for each donor? Yes = 2 pts.　　No = 0 pts.	

QUESTIONS	POINTS
19 Do you list the names of husbands and wives separately (John and Mary Brown)? Yes = 2 pts. No = 0 pts.	
20 Does your fundraising staff actively plan for and build into their plans regular stewardship calls or *moves*? Yes = 3 pts. No = 0 pts.	
21 Do you publish a CEO letter or newsletter which is sent every 4 weeks to a small select list of major gift donors, prospects, and influentials? Every 4 weeks = 4 pts. Quarterly = 2 pts. Sent, but not on a regular basis = 1 pt. Not sent out = 0 pts.	
22 Do you publish a newsletter or magazine which is mailed to your donors which provides major space for stories about donors and gives recognition for their gifts? Yes = 2 pts. No = 0 pts.	

QUESTIONS	POINTS
23　How often are these published? Quarterly = 3 pts. Semi-annually = 2 pts. Annually = 1 pt.	
24　Does your staff actively discuss stewardship activities and at least annually review stewardship plans and activities? Yes = 2 pts.　　　　No = 0 pts.	
25　Are stewardship activities built into your budgeting process so there are funds for an active program? Yes = 2 pts.　　　　No = 0 pts.	
26　Has your organization conducted a donor survey or held donor focus group sessions in the past 24 months? Yes = 2 pts.　　　　No = 0 pts.	

QUESTIONS	POINTS
27 **Does your organization regularly survey currently lapsed donors to determine the reasons they might have dropped out?** Yes = 2 pts. No = 0 pts.	
28 **Do you (or would you) proactively communicate with your donors about organizational changes or issues even though they may be somewhat unpleasant or sensitive?** Yes = 1 pt. No = 0 pts.	
29 **Do you have gift clubs or levels where you recognize donors for their cumulative giving?** Yes = 2 pts. No = 0 pts.	
30 **Do you consistently provide donor recognition through such things as gift clubs, *walls of honor*, signage, dinners and/or receptions, etc.?** Yes = 2 pts. No = 0 pts.	

QUESTIONS	POINTS
31 Do you have a Heritage group (or a name of some sort) that provides recognition for those who have made a planned gift or have provided for you in their estate plans? Yes = 4 pts. No = 0 pts.	
32 Do you monitor and evaluate what other charitable organizations are doing in the area of stewardship? Yes = 2 pts. No = 0 pts.	
33 Do you periodically provide *hospitality* and courtesy sessions to support staff and other appropriate staff in order to give them a sense of membership and render them more proactive, courteous, and effective? Yes = 2 pts. No = 0 pts.	

QUESTIONS	POINTS
34 **Do you actively involve major donors through *job shadowing*, taking them on tours, or in some other fashion personally introducing them to the beneficiaries of your service?** Yes = 2 pts. No = 0 pts.	
35 **Do you in some creative fashion reach out to your donors in non-conventional ways through such media as e-mail, web sites, audio tapes, videotapes, etc.?** Yes = 2 pts. No = 0 pts.	
TOTAL:	

III

Studies of
Philanthropy
in Action

"There never was a person who did anything worth doing who did not receive more than he gave."

Henry Ward Beecher

During my years of organizing and presenting training seminars I have learned the value of evaluating case histories. All of the cases I have developed for my seminars are real. That was important to me because I felt that as fundraisers we needed practical information which we could utilize as we practice our craft. "Pie in the sky" situational analyses would not prove useful in my opinion.

A reasonable way to approach a major gift case is in a small group setting. The group is presented with the scenario and then asked to discuss the situation and develop a strategy. The most meaningful context is that of the moves management process (see *The Artful Journey*). That is, you can ask yourself the following questions:

- Who are the natural partners? Why do you consider them natural partners? What will their respective roles be?

- Who are your primary players and why do you feel they have the maximum leverage?

- What will your next two to three moves be? What are your objectives for each move, considering best possible and minimum acceptable outcomes?

The cases to follow were carefully selected because they illustrate situations most major gifts fundraisers will confront at one time or another. Of course, the names have been changed as have some of the specifics involved, but it is important to remember that the situations actually occurred. Each case will be presented in its entirety, followed by a few comments or questions designed to stimulate your thinking. In the final section of this book are the actual outcomes of these given situations. I told you they were real! Of course, most of the relationships have evolved further from the outcome presented, which superbly illustrates what major gifts fundraising is all about. We build and maintain relationships throughout our donors' entire giving histories with our respective institutions. Some object lessons are common to all of the cases, and I will present these at the close of the chapter. Now to our cases. I sincerely hope you find them to be as instructive as I have.

The Case of the Elusive Fundraising Strategy

As the Director of Development at a medium-sized university, you spend much of your time thinking strategically about potential donors. Few are as challenging as Dave and Marcy Schultz. Dave graduated from your institution many years ago, Marcy attended elsewhere. He is 76, she is seven years younger. They both think highly of your university but have had little involvement with it.

What makes the Schultzes so challenging is the psychological setting. He is a workaholic who still spends about 60 hours every week at the office. He is a successful stockbroker, but he has extensive personal holdings that he manages, including several farms and a couple of thousand acres of real estate (Dave was always commenting how illiquid he was). You were told by a reliable source that they are worth from $10.0 to $15.0 million. You've visited with Dave in his office several times, and to your amazement he keeps all of his valuable business documents locked in a safe by his desk. He distrusts most attorneys and accountants. Dave once mentioned to you that someone told him he would have to pay "millions" in estate taxes and that upset him very much. When asked, he offered that they had old wills ("Ma and Pa"), but was too busy now to do anything about it. He said he never went for estate planning advice because he was too busy, didn't want to pay hefty fees, and didn't "want everyone to know what I have." There is one son, Jeff, age 40, married with one child, and he earns a modest living as a teacher. The relationship among the family members is quite good.

As you consider a strategy for the Schultzes, you remind yourself of a few unrelated items which somehow will affect the outcome of the relationship between the Schultzes and your university. The problem is, you need to determine how everything fits together and that is not simple. You consider:

- The Schultzes have little giving experience. They made a gift a few years ago to their local library. The amount was $100,000, and you thought it was overkill that the library named a wing in their honor. However, Dave and Marcy loved it!

- Dave once confessed to you that he works so hard because he is afraid of losing everything. "Look at what has happened to the Hunts" is a favorite admonition.

- Dave can be difficult to work with because he has a short attention span. He is always trying to move on to the next business item. You have found it is necessary to meet with the Schultzes after the markets close in the afternoon, and Saturday mornings (before Dave goes to work about noon) are often best.

- The Schultzes, especially Marcy, love attention from important people.

- Neither Dave nor Marcy understand much about universities. Terms like endowment and Professorship mean nothing to them, and Dave doesn't seem that interested in programmatic issues anyway.

You know you must plan a strategy and make some "moves." You pick up your pen and stare at your legal pad. What will you write under your heading, "Strategy for Dave and Marcy Schultz?"

What do you think we are dealing with regarding the Schultzes' attitude toward philanthropy? Might there be an accumulation vs. distribution issue, and, if so, what does this imply for your strategy? Does it help or hinder your efforts that the Schultzes received a wonderful naming opportunity for a relatively modest gift? If you ponder these and other questions, you will be well on your way toward settling upon the next two or three steps with the Schultzes.

See page 69 for the outcome of this case study.

This next case presents some rather subtle challenges. I am quite familiar with what happened in this situation and can assure you that a careful and considered approach was important.

The Case of the Disillusioned and Confused Prospects

—

The Successful Turnaround

Background:

As the Major Gifts Director at a medium-sized hospital, you schedule a dinner meeting with some prospects who give annually to your organization and who appear greatly interested in its work. Ostensibly, they have the economic means to give at a much higher level. These prospects benefited directly and significantly from the fine work of a staff surgeon some years ago and that is the basis for their continuing involvement with your hospital.

You are vaguely aware that your predecessor at the hospital spent a great deal of time with these prospects a couple of years ago. The topic of discussion at that time was the development of a hospice program for which $150,000 of private funding would have been of great value. That proposal never went anywhere, and you later learned that just prior to his departure your predecessor told the head of the oncology unit that he was sure these prospects would donate $250,000 to further an active program of clinical research.

Your dinner with the prospects was pleasant, but it was obvious your predecessor misread the situation badly. To your horror, you learn the following:

- The prospects had expressed only a general interest in the hospice concept and they would never consider direct financial support. Hospice was just not that important to them.

- The prospects told your predecessor that oncology was an important area, but they also indicated that there were other programs of much greater interest to them. They were chagrined when the oncology head proposed a gift.

- The prospects are interested in supporting your organization, but they stated that it might take a few years before they are ready to offer major support because their business consumed a great deal of cash.

- Your prospects asked what happened to the $20,000 they gave last year. Your predecessor was to get back to them with some ideas and failed to do so.

- The prospects indicate that they have observed other gift announcements at your hospital and think it is very exciting when donors have something named in their honor. They indicate that it would be fun to someday know that something was permanently named for them.

Other Facts:

- The prospects are a married couple, ages 60 and 62;
- the prospects had never made a major gift (i.e., above $10,000) before the $20,000;
- the prospects have no children.

Questions to Stimulate Your Thinking:

What do you tell your prospects now?

What's your strategy?

Timetable?

What about the $20,000?

How do your turn their distress to excitement?

How important is it that you unearth what happened with their $20,000 gift? What is your recommendation if you discover that the gift was utilized as unrestricted support for the hospital? Will you distinguish between short-term and long-term strategies? What principles of cultivation and stewardship are involved and what might they imply about turning around the relationship with these prospects?

See page 75 for the outcome of this case study.

Sometimes situations aren't particularly complex, but a plan that reflects perseverance and consistency is a challenge to develop and implement. This is often where packaging becomes important, especially where there is some degree of urgency because of age. With all of this in mind, consider the situation with our friend, Larry Davis.

The Case of the Family Legacy — Building a Tradition of Giving

A s the Director of Development at a major hospital and research center you find yourself contemplating what you believe to be a potential major gift opportunity. The object of your thoughts is Larry Davis, age 82, a long-time friend to your organization.

You don't know for sure, but you have reason to believe that Larry's net worth is approximately $10.0 million. You also remind yourself that Larry has three ex-wives, presumably well taken care of by now, and two children, both of whom are mature and ostensibly quite successful. You are ever mindful of the fact that Larry thinks very highly of your CEO and his wife, and, in fact, he annually invites them to spend some time with him on his yacht in Florida. Larry used to be close to several board members, but all of them are deceased. Larry has never forgotten how much he enjoyed hosting the CEO and his wife for a party on the yacht, with the guest list comprised of hospital friends and compiled with your input. Larry is an inveterate "name-dropper," and he likes to tell others of the mayors, college presidents and powerful hospital directors he knows personally. He regales in telling others how many times, and by whom, he has been solicited for major gifts.

Larry and his family have generously supported your institution over the years. Approximately 20 years ago his father funded a research laboratory ($50,000 gift) in pediatrics, the research in which has focused on infant mortality. Though he never discussed the issue with his father, Larry presumes the gift was motivated by his older brother's death due to Sudden Infant Death Syndrome. Five years ago Larry made a gift of $150,000 which established an endowment fund to support research in the lab.

You wonder what to do next with Larry. A new center is being constructed adjacent to the hospital which will house research and an intensive care area. The new facility is due primarily to the generosity ($8.0 million) of a donor whose name will be honored on the facility. You know of Larry's strong interest in and identification with pediatrics at your hospital, and you are equally cognizant of his advancing age. Does the new research/intensive care facility offer an opportunity? If so, how should you proceed? What about the bigger picture — Larry's estate? He makes no secret of the fact that he no longer feels much of an obligation to the kids. He also mentions an interest in other charities, and further obscuring the issue is the fact that Larry has reached his tax deduction limit this year and for the next three years. Where do you go from here?

How might you tie together short-term with long-term possibilities in Larry's case? Could something be done to use a short-term outcome as cultivation for a greater opportunity for the long-term? Might this be a situation where the natural partner relationship is critical? Consider all of these issues carefully before reaching a conclusion and then compare it to the actual outcome provided in the appendix.

See page 79 for the outcome of this case study.

And now let's really have some fun! How about the gift opportunity of a career?! How would you handle the following?

The Case of the Mega-Prospect: The Opportunity for the Ultimate Gift of a Career

Background:

As the newly appointed Director of Development at a major university, you are furiously reviewing your prospect database for names of those requiring special attention. The fundraising program has been relatively passive over the years, and a major gifts program is acutely needed. Your board and CEO are eager to initiate a major capital campaign. The good news is that you have uncovered some marvelous prospects, but the bad news is that few have been properly cultivated. Thus, they are not giving at the level merited by their capabilities.

One name really stands out in your prospect review. A few years ago this prospect sold his company to a Fortune 500 firm for $400 million. He is a graduate of your institution (Ph.D. in Physics), but his only contacts over the years have been with some departmental faculty who are conducting research in areas of interest. However, he has fond memories of his days at your institution and attributes much of his success to his Ph.D.

Other Facts:

- Your prospect is strongly oriented toward the sciences and research.

- He has already made a $20 million gift to another university for a science library.

- He has expressed a desire to give away his fortune before he dies.

- He believes that this country is falling behind in the sciences and that we need to be creative in order to be "on the cutting edge."

- One of your board members knows him on a business basis as they are both directors of a Fortune 500 firm.

- Your prospect is 74 years old.

- He most enjoys contacts with bright faculty members and especially enjoys conversing with young, "bright" professors.

Questions to Stimulate Your Thinking:

What is your game plan?

Who do you involve?

How many steps are involved?

What is your time frame?

What will you be seeking?

What kind of timetable is reasonable with a prospect of this magnitude? Is it important to have some interim giving steps before seeking what you consider to be the maximum possible contribution? Who would you involve in determining the giving opportunities to be presented? Could you do some probing with pre-proposal presentations along the way? How do you maintain momentum while not jeopardizing an opportunity because of your own sense of urgency? While your institution's mega prospect may have far more modest giving potential than our friend in this case, the issue is not really dollar magnitude. Rather, it is one of strategizing, nurturing and timing. It would be fun to join your discussion of this particular opportunity.

See page 83 for the outcome of this case study.

See page 83 for the outcome of this case study.

You will find it intriguing to compare your answers to the actual outcomes, but I urge you not to do so until you have had a thorough discussion of the possibilities involved. Once you compare your responses to what actually occurred, the object lessons will become clear. All of these cases demonstrate the following major gifts fundraising principles:

- Major gifts fundraising is more of an art than a science. There is no one path to the same successful outcome. In other words, there really isn't a right or wrong answer to any particular case.

- You should trust the process. While information is incomplete and outcomes uncertain, if you work the moves management process the mosaic begins to take shape. That is, if you establish objectives for your moves and demonstrate active listening during your calls, the answers you need will be forthcoming. The process really works.

- You should trust your instincts. Of course, experience helps hone your instinctive intuitions. But whatever your stage of experience, if you combine active listening with an acute probing of your own instinctive conclusions you can be confident of heading in the right direction.

- Another important object lesson is that you should work as a team. The strategy team for a given prospect is composed of all of the natural partners, and you should actively collaborate with your colleagues and volunteers. You can glean a lot of information from both staff and volunteer natural partners, and you can count on the fact that your strategies and decisions will be improved mightily if you initiate an active dialogue. On an informal basis you can even consult with other fundraisers who have had similar cases in order to benefit from their experiences and insights. I know that in my office this is something we actively pursue as colleagues, and I can assure you it has improved our results. Let's also remember to be open to the input of staff and volunteer natural partners who do not have professional fundraising experience. Some-

times their insights in a given situation will be keen-
er than ours, which should not be a problem if we
take satisfaction in the fundraising results which
touch lives and not in self-glory.

As a final bit of mental stimulation, why not consider a
case for which there is not yet an outcome. It is ongoing.
How would you handle this case?

The Case of the Burgeoning Giving Relationship and the Importance of Timing

Background:

As the Director of Major and Planned Gifts for a major healthcare agency you are contemplating your strategy for Jerry Thomas.

Jerry is a wildly successful investment banker. At age 45 he is already worth millions. The strongest connection to your organization is his friendship with the doctor who oversees research funding in a particular area. His family (i.e., his father) was affected in a very direct way by the disease your agency seeks to eradicate, although, interestingly enough, his friend's particular area of emphasis is not directly related to the family affliction. It's just that he likes this person (Dr. Mary Davis) so much he has supported your agency to the tune of $400,000. The support was in the form of two gifts of $200,000 which were designated for Dr. Davis' area.

While Jerry is fabulously wealthy, he is also very young. You guess his current net worth is $35 million. His annual gross income exceeds $2 million and is growing. He is used to dealing at the highest levels of corporate society, but he has never even met the members of the agency's rather prestigious board. Despite his wealth, he is concerned about his next acquisition whenever you talk with him. He also dotes on his two teenage sons and wonders aloud where they will attend college and what he can do to help them. His wife has been ill of late and it appears to be chronic.

It is obvious that Jerry enjoys your focus luncheons featuring various researchers. This is particularly so when the focus is the area which affected his family, and he seemed to like the doctor who heads this division at your agency. Still, there is his friendship with Mary Davis to consider. But you know that research funding for her division is already adequate and of low priority in terms of impact.

Your $100 million capital campaign just got underway and your boss thinks you should ask Jerry for a $10 million gift. After all, he is very capable. You wonder if that might be too much, too soon.

Questions to Stimulate Your Thinking:

What is your strategy?

What are your next moves?

Who do you involve?

Is Jerry a candidate for a campaign gift? If so, for what and how much?

   You ponder your answers as you prepare for the next campaign strategy session.

I believe these cases vividly illustrate the complexity and the richness involved in the relationship building enterprise. People are infinitely complex and fascinating, and we become better fundraisers when we cease looking for specificity where it just does not exist. We must be open to the process. I hope these exercises make that point and encourage you to march forward boldly, confident that you will succeed. What I have discovered is that if you take people of integrity (you and the other natural partners involved in the process) and put them together with a compelling cause and caring prospects, good things are sure to follow.

Finally, we should always remember that actually working the process is what will ensure results. We must settle upon our strategies and then make the calls. If we do so, success will follow. The cases and the other tools provided in this book will undoubtedly be of most help to those who are committed to implementation.

IV

Case Study Outcomes

"Philanthropy is the rent we pay for the joy and privilege we have for our space on this earth."

Jerold Panas

The Case of the Elusive Fundraising Strategy

The strategy that was developed for the Schultzes was long-term in nature. In fact, it was implemented over a three to four year period. This was necessitated by the nature of Dave's personality, in combination with the Schultzes' lack of awareness of your institution, the complexity of the plan, and their very limited philanthropic experience.

The strategy consisted of two elements: cultivation and estate planning service. As to the latter, given all the facts it was not likely that an emphasis on a large outright gift would be productive, and even a smaller gift to involve and cultivate might prove difficult given Dave's constant concern about financial survival and his complaints about illiquidity. Dave seemed concerned about estate taxes, and going "down the path of least resistance" (or greater interest) seemed to make sense.

Besides, estate plan provisions are often psychologically easier to secure than outright gifts and you wanted to be sure to maximize the potential commitment. Your Director of Deferred Giving was introduced to Dave and Marcy and the "chemistry" was great. Over a three year period a series of Saturday morning meetings took place where the Schultzes were introduced to diagrammed estate plan options which focused on their son, Jeff, and tax savings through charitable provisions. The Director of Deferred Giving used an agreed upon figure of $15.0 million in his illustrations, without requiring an estate inventory and emphasizing the fact that "it could all be lost — or doubled — tomorrow and that's why the flexibility of an estate plan vs. lifetime actions is preferred."

The cultivation plan involved many contacts over the three year period, with several involving the president of the university. For example, the president and his wife had dinner with the Schultzes at a club in their town and hosted them on campus several times. As "luck would have it," attending one of the president's parties was an author whom Dave greatly admired. Dave and Marcy were also provided an opportunity to visit the College of Commerce building where Dave took some classes, and they were shown the plans for a new building and some major renovation.

The Director of Deferred Giving secured the Schultzes' agreement on an estate plan and accompanied them on a visit to an attorney he helped them find. This took some persuading, but Dave was often reminded of the tax savings to be had. The attorney was briefed prior to the visit. Trusts and wills were signed resulting in a commitment of from $5.0 to $6.0 million.

Shortly after the wills were signed the Director of Deferred Giving suggested a meeting with the president to determine what wonderful and exciting things could be done with the Schultzes' future support, presuming, of course, that it's not lost first!

The real involvement and excitement for the Schultzes was thus begun, and the result will be the "Dave and Marcy

Schultz Center for Entrepreneurship" in a new commerce building which is now under construction. Partial lifetime funding of the Center is now under discussion.

The Case of the Disillusioned and Confused Prospects

Steps Taken:

- The $20,000 gift from the prior year is put into a fund bearing the prospects' names, and this fund is left to accumulate interest. That is, you conveyed to the prospects that their $20,000 and the interest thereon is to be held until a determination can be made as to how it is to be used.

- It is suggested that the $20,000 be combined with whatever gifts might be made over the next few years such that their total support could be applied directly to the program of greatest interest. It is further suggested that the staff should work with the prospects to explore and select that program of greatest interest, and that the process would be more enjoyable and accurate because there was no time pressure. That is, they were a few years away from making their major gift and the luxury of time would result in a better outcome. In the meantime, the $20,000 would grow in value such that additional leverage would be applied in the chosen direction.

- The CEO of the hospital is enlisted to assist in the cultivation of the prospects and to search for the program of greatest interest. Prominent naming opportunities are to be emphasized.

- Numerous cultivation contacts occur over the next three years.

Ultimate Outcome:

Three years later, pursuant to unwinding a business interest, the prospects make a $250,000 commitment, payable over five years, to the hospital. A permanent endowment fund is established with the income used for unrestricted purposes, and in return, a physical therapy room is named in honor of the donors. The couple enjoys the formal naming ceremony and takes pleasure in the copper plaque bearing their likeness next to the entrance to the room.

The Case of the Family Legacy

As a first step, the CEO and his wife visit Larry in Florida. The objective of this "move" is strictly cultivation.

A gala party is held upon Larry's yacht (with a carefully crafted invitation list) and the CEO and spouse spend two days with Larry cruising the Florida coast.

The follow-up to the party occurs 30 days later when the CEO pays Larry a specially planned visit, along with the major gifts officer. The CEO is asked to handle the call alone but says he prefers to have a fundraiser along. The meeting takes place over lunch at a club for which the CEO has reciprocal privileges.

During the meeting the CEO seeks from Larry a $1.0 million commitment for a pediatric intensive care unit in the new center. During the course of the presentation the CEO leans over, places his hand on Larry's arm, and says, "It would be a personal favor to me if you would consider a gift to make possible the Davis Pediatric Intensive Care Unit. It's vital, and we now have the opportunity to make the dream come true because of the new facility. The Davis name is synonymous with pediatric care at our hospital, and so we turn to you again."

A proposal was left and two follow-up visits with the major gifts officer occurred. The major gifts officer stressed how much the gift meant to the CEO and indicated the urgency in reaching a decision because planning for the new facility was moving forward at a rapid pace. Further, the issue of the deduction limit was reviewed, and it was agreed that payments could begin in three years with completion in six and a guarantee through Larry's estate plan. A $1.0 million commitment was made, and thirty days thereafter Larry paid the pledge in full, notwithstanding caveats about deductibility. Larry just thought it was "cleaner" and would help the CEO if he "stepped forward" now.

As to the long-term, "moves" are underway. The grand announcement of Larry's gift at a hospital gala, highlighted by dinners with the CEO and his wife, were major cultivational steps. At the current time, another party on board Larry's yacht is being planned. Subsequent to this cultivation the CEO will seek from Larry an estate plan commitment of $2.5 million to endow the "Davis Center for Pediatric Care and Well Being." This gift will be presented as the capstone of two generations of Davis family philanthropy to the hospital. The Center will, of course, house the Davis Lab, Davis pediatric research and the Davis Pediatric Intensive Care Unit.

The Case of the Mega-Prospect

Steps Taken:

- Extensive cultivation is undertaken with the first step involving a visit from your president and the board member who has a peer relationship. Pursuant to that initial visit a leading research scientist from campus interacts with the prospect and conveys an invitation to visit campus. The visit to campus occurs and the prospect spends time with the president and in the labs with faculty members. Additional cultivational contacts, involving the president and key academic figures, take place on a planned basis.

- 1½ years later the prospect is solicited for a capital campaign leadership gift of $5.0 million. The proposal entails a gift for endowment to support young faculty researchers. The outcome is a $5.0 million leadership gift.

- Over the next 18 months the prospect's gift is announced as a challenge at several gatherings of donors and campaign volunteers. The prospect is asked to talk about why he gave and what the university has meant to him (note the involvement).

- A "blue-ribbon" faculty committee is secretly convened to identify the most exciting opportunity for a scientific project of significant magnitude.
- The challenge is satisfied when the donor's campaign gift of $5.0 million is matched.
- The capital campaign reaches a successful conclusion.
- Six years after the first gift, a $50.0 million proposal for a research center is placed before the prospect. The research center will house both physical and biological research scientists in an effort to understand and simulate human intelligence. The center will be of national and international importance in advancing the sciences.

Ultimate Outcome:

A $40.0 million gift to establish an institute named for your donor is conveyed. The conditions for the gift include a requirement that the others contribute $10.0 million toward the project and that very specific deadlines for the securing of the architect and completion of the building be met. The Institute is dedicated three years later.

Food for Thought:

What opportunities does the Institute provide relative to cultivation in search of the next mega-gift?

Oliver Wendell Holmes, Sr., said, "A moment's insight is sometimes worth a life's experience." I hope that the insights you gain from these case studies will assist you and the wonderful organizations you represent.

Index

William Sturtevant is a nationally recognized specialist in major and deferred gift planning and solicitation strategies. His presentations and seminars are extremely popular and he is a frequent speaker before development professionals, hospital groups, and civic organizations. He has been listed in *Who's Who* and in 1995 was honored as Planned Giving Professional of the Year by *Planned Giving Today*.

He authored *The Artful Journey: Cultivating and Soliciting the Major Gift*, which was published in 1997. An all-time best seller, *The Artful Journey* is considered a must-read by experts in the field.

He is currently Vice President-Trust Relations and Planned Giving at the University of Illinois Foundation, a position he has held since 1980. He played a key role in the University's first capital campaign, as well as its most recent $1 billion campaign. Bill has been directly involved in well over $300 million in major gifts during his tenure at Illinois.

In addition, Sturtevant is a board member of several family charitable foundations and at Strategic Capital Bancorp.

Bill's guiding tenet is that dedication to the best interests of our donors is the only way to achieve the objectives of the charitable organizations we serve.